Published in 2004, 2010 by The Rosen Publishing Group, Inc.
29 East 21st Street, New York, NY 10010

Revised Edition

Book Design: Michael J. Flynn

Photo Credits: Cover © Topham/The Image Works; pp. 4–5 © Bettmann/Corbis; pp. 6–7 (longship) ©
John Connell/Index Stock; p. 7 (Gokstad ship) © Richard T. Nowitz/Corbis; pp. 11, 14–15, 20 (swords
and ax), 21 © Ted Spiegel/Corbis; pp. 13, 17 © Gianni Dagli Orti/Corbis; pp. 18–19 © Hulton-Deutsch
Collection/Corbis.

Library of Congress Cataloging-in-Publication Data

Levy, Janey.
          At sea on a Viking ship : solving problems of
length and weight using the four math operations / Janey
Levy.
                    p. cm. -- (PowerMath)
          Includes index.
          Summary: This book uses four mathematical
operations to describe the Vikings' ships and the Vikings'
way of life.
  ISBN 978-0-8239-8977-5 (hardcover)
  ISBN 978-0-8239-8922-5 (pbk)
  ISBN 978-0-8239-7450-4 (6-pack)
          1. Mensuration—Juvenile literature   2. Arithmetic—
Juvenile literature   3. Vikings—Juvenile literature
[1. Measurement   2. Arithmetic   3. Vikings]   I. Title
II. Series
               2004
          513.2--dc21

Manufactured in the United States of America

CPSIA Compliance Information: Batch #CR01503ORC: For further information contact Rosen Publishing, New York, New York at 1-800-237-9932.

Contents

The Vikings

The Vikings were adventurous sailors from the parts of northern Europe that are now called Norway, Sweden, and Denmark. Their long, narrow ships traveled smoothly even through rough, stormy seas. Around 800 A.D., Vikings began to make long sea journeys to distant places. The Vikings were **raiders**, but they were also **explorers**, traders, and settlers. Vikings explored the east coast of North America around 1000 A.D., almost 500 years before Columbus reached the New World.

The Vikings had to take food, water, **weapons**, and other supplies on their journeys. They had to be sure the weight of the supplies wasn't more than their ship could carry. Let's take a look at what life was like on a Viking ship. We can use addition, subtraction, multiplication, and division to help us understand it.

At Sea on a Viking Ship

lving Problems of Length and Weight Using the Four Math Operations

Janey Levy

Math *for the* **REAL World**™

Rosen
Classroom™

New York

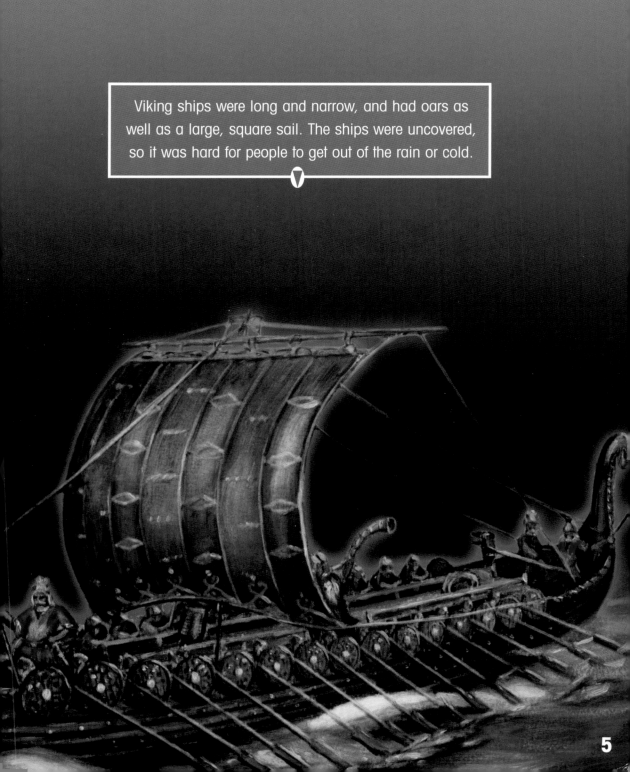

Viking ships were long and narrow, and had oars as well as a large, square sail. The ships were uncovered, so it was hard for people to get out of the rain or cold.

Longships and Knarrs

The most famous kind of Viking ship was called a longship. The Vikings used longships for raids and fighting. After they died, wealthy Vikings were buried in their longships with things they thought they would need in the next life. Beds, food, tools, and weapons have been found in buried longships.

In 1880, a longship used to bury a Viking chief was found at Gokstad, Norway. The Gokstad ship is about 76 feet long and 17 feet wide.

Between 1957 and 1962, parts of five Viking ships were found in a narrow bay near Copenhagen, Denmark. One of them was a small longship. It was about 20 feet shorter than the Gokstad ship and 8 feet narrower. How long and wide was the small longship? To find out, subtract 20 feet from the length of the Gokstad ship and 8 feet from its width.

Gokstad ship ▶

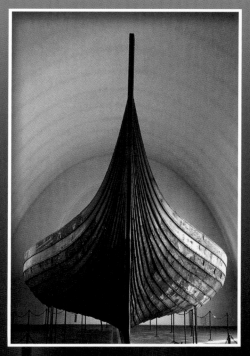

Length

```
   76  feet (length of Gokstad ship)
 – 20  feet
 ─────
   56  feet (length of Copenhagen ship)
```

The Copenhagen longship was 56 feet long.

Width

```
   17  feet (width of Gokstad ship)
 –  8  feet
 ─────
    9  feet (width of Copenhagen ship)
```

The Copenhagen longship was 9 feet wide.

▲ **longship**

One of the other ships found in the bay was a knarr, a type of ship the Vikings used for trading and exploring. The knarr was about the same length as the small longship, but it was much wider. The knarr was about 54 feet long and about 15 feet wide. How much wider was it than the small longship? You can subtract 9 feet from 15 feet to get your answer.

$$
\begin{array}{r}
15 \text{ feet (width of knarr)} \\
- \quad 9 \text{ feet (width of Copenhagen longship)} \\
\hline
6 \text{ feet}
\end{array}
$$

The knarr was 6 feet wider than
the Copenhagen longship.

Longships were narrow because that made it easier for them to move quickly during a battle. Knarrs were wider because that gave them more room for livestock and objects for trade.

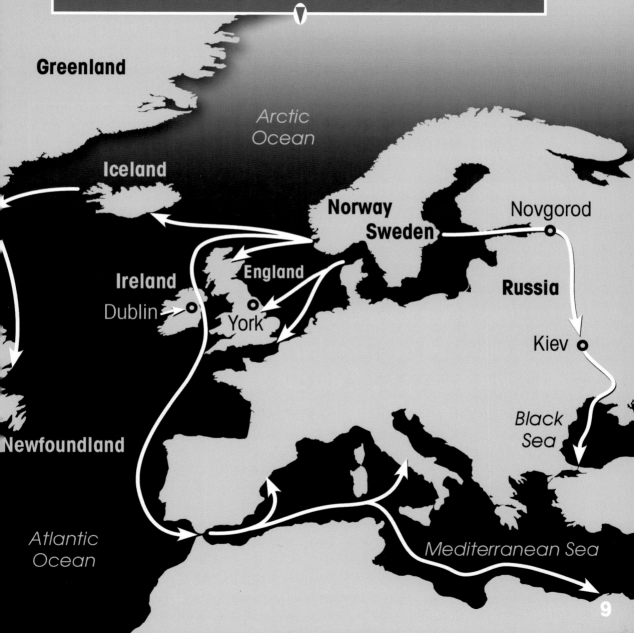

This map shows the paths followed by Viking ships. Vikings founded Dublin, Ireland, around 840 A.D. In 862 A.D. they founded Novgorod, Russia, and 4 years later they set up a kingdom in York, England. Vikings began to settle in Iceland around 870 A.D.

Greenland

Arctic Ocean

Iceland

Norway
Sweden

Novgorod

Ireland
England
Dublin
York

Russia

Kiev

Newfoundland

Black Sea

Atlantic Ocean

Mediterranean Sea

A knarr's large, square sail helped to move the ship across the sea. It also had oars that were used when the knarr entered or left a harbor. A longship also had a sail, but the oars were probably used more often. With oars, it was easier to change direction quickly during a battle. It was not always possible to do this using a sail.

The Gokstad ship had 16 oars on each side. How many oars did it have altogether? You can multiply 16 by 2 to get your answer. The Gokstad ship had a total of 32 oars.

$$
\begin{array}{r}
1 \\
16 \text{ oars} \\
\times\ \ 2 \text{ sides} \\
\hline
32 \text{ oars}
\end{array}
$$

The longest longship ever found had a total of 68 oars! How many oars did it have on each side? You can divide 68 by 2 to get your answer.
This ship had 34 oars on each side!

$$
\begin{array}{r}
34 \text{ oars} \\
2\,)\overline{\,68} \\
-\,6 \\
\hline
08 \\
-\,8 \\
\hline
0
\end{array}
$$

How many more oars did this longship have on each side than the Gokstad ship? Subtract 16 from 34 to get your answer. This longship had 18 more oars on each side than the Gokstad ship.

$$
\begin{array}{r}
\overset{2}{\cancel{3}}\,\overset{1}{4} \text{ oars} \\
-\ 16 \text{ oars} \\
\hline
18 \text{ oars}
\end{array}
$$

In modern times, many people have built copies of Viking longships. Some people have even crossed the Atlantic Ocean from Europe to North America in their longship!

Historians believe the Gokstad ship could handle a total weight of 40,000 pounds. That included the crew and their weapons, food and other supplies, and the weight of the ship itself. Let's do the math to see how this works out.

Vikings built the Gokstad ship from the wood of oak, spruce, and pine trees. They used 13,530 pounds of oak. The spruce and pine used in the ship weighed 2,431 pounds altogether. How many total pounds of wood were used in the Gokstad ship? You can add 13,530 and 2,431 to get your answer.

$$
\begin{array}{r}
13{,}530 \ \text{pounds (oak)} \\
+ \quad 2{,}431 \ \text{pounds (spruce and pine)} \\
\hline
15{,}961 \ \text{pounds}
\end{array}
$$

There were 15,961 pounds of wood used to build the Gokstad ship.

This picture was sewn on cloth around 1040 A.D. It shows men cutting down trees to use in building ships. The man on the right has begun to shape a cut tree into the boards needed to build a ship.

The Gokstad ship's **rigging** and wool sail weighed 2,200 pounds. Iron was also used in the ship. The nails were made of iron and so was the **anchor**. The rigging and sail weighed 4 times as much as the iron used in the ship. How many pounds of iron were used? You can divide 2,200 by 4 to get your answer.

$$
\begin{array}{r}
550 \text{ pounds} \\
4\overline{)2{,}200} \\
-20 \\
\hline
20 \\
-20 \\
\hline
0
\end{array}
$$

All the iron in the ship weighed 550 pounds. If the anchor weighed 220 pounds, how much did all the iron nails weigh? You can subtract 220 from 550 to get your answer.

$$
\begin{array}{r}
550 \text{ pounds} \\
-\ 220 \text{ pounds} \\
\hline
330 \text{ pounds}
\end{array}
$$

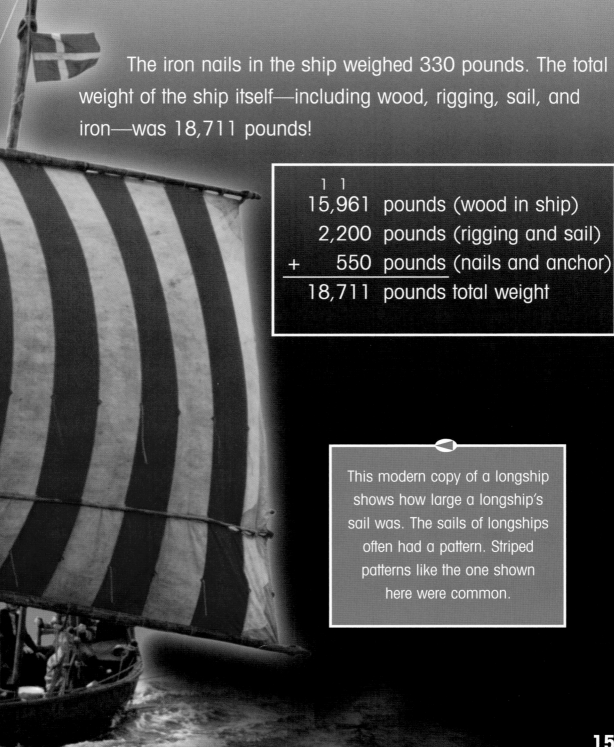

The iron nails in the ship weighed 330 pounds. The total weight of the ship itself—including wood, rigging, sail, and iron—was 18,711 pounds!

```
        1 1
   15,961  pounds (wood in ship)
    2,200  pounds (rigging and sail)
+     550  pounds (nails and anchor)
   18,711  pounds total weight
```

This modern copy of a longship shows how large a longship's sail was. The sails of longships often had a pattern. Striped patterns like the one shown here were common.

The Gokstad ship probably had a crew of about 70 men, including 64 men who took turns rowing and 1 man who **steered** the ship. If each man weighed 175 pounds, what was the total weight of all the crew members? You can multiply 175 by 70 to get your answer. The total weight of the crew was 12,250 pounds.

$$
\begin{array}{rl}
^{5\,3}\quad & \\
175 & \text{pounds} \\
\times\ 70 & \text{men} \\
\hline
0 & \\
+\ 12\,25 & \\
\hline
12{,}250 & \text{pounds}
\end{array}
$$

To find the total weight of the ship and the crew, you can add the total weight of the ship (18,711 pounds) and the total weight of the crew (12,250 pounds). The total weight of the ship and crew was 30,961 pounds.

$$
\begin{array}{rl}
^{1}\quad & \\
18{,}711 & \text{pounds} \\
+\ 12{,}250 & \text{pounds} \\
\hline
30{,}961 & \text{pounds}
\end{array}
$$

There was no way to cook food on a crowded longship. The Vikings had to take food that had been dried, so that it would last for a long time.

The ship had to carry food and drinking water for the entire crew. The Gokstad ship probably carried a total of 3,300 pounds of water. It carried about 30 pounds of food for each crewman. How many pounds of food did the ship carry altogether? You can multiply 30 by 70 to get your answer.

$$\begin{array}{r} 30 \text{ pounds (food)} \\ \times\ 70 \text{ men} \\ \hline 0 \\ +\ 210 \\ \hline 2{,}100 \text{ pounds of food} \end{array}$$

If we add the weights of the food and water, we find that the Gokstad ship carried 5,400 pounds of food and water for its crew.

```
  2,100    pounds (food)
+ 3,300    pounds (water)
─────────
  5,400    pounds of food and water
```

What was the total weight of the ship, crew, food, and water? You can add the combined weight of the ship and crew found on page 16 to the combined weight of the food and water to get your answer.

```
   1
  30,961    pounds (ship and crew)
+  5,400    pounds (food and water)
──────────
  36,361    pounds
```

Vikings on a longship needed their weapons as much as they needed food and water. Their weapons included **swords**, axes, and **shields**.

Vikings hung their shields on the sides of their longships, as we see in this photo of a modern copy of a longship.

Viking swords and axes were made of iron, so they were very heavy. Crew members stored their weapons and other personal things in private chests. Each man was allowed to bring 44 pounds of weapons and personal objects. What was the total weight of these things on the Gokstad ship if there were 70 men on board? You can multiply 44 by 70 to get your answer.

$$
\begin{array}{r}
{}^{2}\\
44 \text{ pounds}\\
\times \quad 70 \text{ men}\\
\hline
0\\
+\ 308\\
\hline
3{,}080 \text{ pounds}
\end{array}
$$

There were 3,080 pounds of weapons and personal objects.

Viking swords ▼

Viking ax ▼

Now we've studied the Gokstad ship, its crew, and all the things the crew needed to take with them. It's time to add the final figures to see how much the ship weighed when it was fully loaded. To get the grand total, add the combined weight of the ship, crew, food, and water from page 18 to the weight of weapons and personal objects from page 20.

$$
\begin{array}{r}
\overset{1}{36{,}361} \text{ pounds (ship, crew, food, and water)} \\
+\ \ 3{,}080 \text{ pounds (weapons and personal objects)} \\
\hline
39{,}441 \text{ pounds}
\end{array}
$$

The total weight of the fully loaded ship was 39,441 pounds. That's more than 2 school buses weigh!

The Viking Age Ends

The Viking age came to an end around 1050 A.D., as other groups defeated the Vikings in battle and took over their lands. However, the Vikings have not been forgotten. In addition to their accomplishments as explorers, they created many beautiful artworks, poems, and stories. Vikings even gave us the names for three of our days of the week! Wednesday is named for Odin, the main Viking god. Thursday is named for Thor, the Viking god of thunder and weather. Friday is named for Freya, the Viking goddess of love and beauty.

Vikings are also honored today for their ideas about the law. In 930 A.D., they set up one of Europe's earliest **parliaments**. They also believed in the right to a **trial by jury**, which is still considered important today.

Glossary

anchor (ANG-kuhr) A heavy metal object on a chain that is tied to a ship. It can be thrown into the water to keep the ship in one place.

explorer (ek-SPLOOR-uhr) Someone who travels to new places to gain knowledge about them.

historian (hih-STOHR-ee-uhn) Someone who studies history.

parliament (PAHR-luh-muhnt) A group of leaders who meet to make laws for a country.

raider (RAY-duhr) Someone who attacks others by surprise in order to steal from them.

rigging (RIH-ging) The lines used on a ship to raise, lower, and change the sail.

shield (SHEELD) An object that someone uses to guard themselves from the enemy's weapons in battle. Viking shields were round.

steer (STEER) To control the direction something goes.

sword (SOHRD) A weapon with a long blade that is sharp on both edges.

trial by jury (TRYUHL BY JUR-ee) A system in which a group of a person's peers decides whether or not the facts prove that the person has done something illegal.

weapon (WEH-puhn) Something like a knife or gun that is used to harm others.

Index